T0243884

LETTER FROM
BIRMINGHAM JAIL

DR. MARTIN LUTHER KING JR.

LETTER FROM BIRMINGHAM JAIL

Afterword by Reginald Dwayne Betts

MartinLuther King Jr. *Library*

**MartinLuther
KingJr.** *Library*

In Association with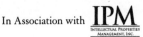

License granted by Intellectual Properties Management, Inc. on behalf of
the Estate of Martin Luther King, Jr., Inc.

HarperCollins books may be purchased for educational, business, or
sales promotional use. For information, please email the Special Markets
Department at SPsales@harpercollins.com.

Art © santima.studio/stock.adobe.com

Library of Congress Cataloging-in-Publication Data has been applied for.

ISBN 978-0-06-342583-5
ISBN 978-0-06-342581-1 (Library Edition)

24 25 26 27 28 LBC 5 4 3 2 1

LETTER FROM BIRMINGHAM JAIL

April 12, 1963

The following is the public statement directed to Martin Luther King Jr. by eight white Alabaman clergymen.

We the undersigned clergymen are among those who, in January, issued "An Appeal for Law and Order and Common Sense" in dealing with racial problems in Alabama. We expressed understanding that honest convictions in racial matters could properly be pursued in the courts, but urged that decisions of those courts should in the meantime be peacefully obeyed.

Since that time there has been some evidence of increased forbearance and a willingness to face facts. Responsible citizens have undertaken to work on various problems which cause racial friction and unrest.

In Birmingham recent public events have given indication that we all have opportunity for a new constructive and realistic approach to racial problems.

However, we are now confronted by a series of demonstrations by some of our Negro citizens, directed and led in part by outsiders. We recognize the natural impatience of people who feel that their hopes are slow in being realized. But we are convinced that these demonstrations are unwise and untimely.

We agree rather with certain local Negro leadership which has called for honest and open negotiation of racial issues in our area.

And we believe this kind of facing of issues can best be accomplished by citizens of our own metropolitan area, white and Negro, meeting with their knowledge and experience of the local situation. All of us need to face that responsibility and find proper channels for its accomplishment.

Just as we formerly pointed out that "hatred and violence have no sanction in our religious and political traditions," we also point out that such actions as incite hatred and violence, however technically peaceful those actions may be, have not contributed to the resolution of our local problems.

We do not believe that these days of new hope are days when extreme measures are justified in Birmingham.

We commend the community as a whole, and the local news media and law enforcement officials in particular, on the calm manner in which these demonstrations have been handled.

We urge the public to continue to show restraint should the demonstrations continue, and the law enforcement officials to remain calm and continue to protect our city from violence.

We further strongly urge our own Negro community to withdraw support from these demonstrations, and to unite locally in working peacefully for a better Birmingham.

When rights are consistently denied, a cause should be pressed in the courts and in negotiations among local leaders, and not in the streets.

We appeal to both our white and Negro citizenry to observe the principles of law and order and common sense.

Bishop C. C. J. Carpenter, Bishop Joseph A. Durick, Rabbi Milton L. Grafman, Bishop Paul Hardin, Bishop Nolan B. Harmon, Rev. George M. Murray, Rev. Edward V. Ramage, and Rev. Earl Stallings

Dr. Martin Luther King Jr. wrote a direct response to the letter from the eight white Alabaman clergymen.

April 16, 1963

My dear Fellow Clergymen,

While confined here in the Birmingham City Jail, I came across your recent statement calling our present activities "unwise and untimely." Seldom, if ever, do I pause to answer criticism of my work and ideas. If I sought to answer all of the criticisms that cross my desk, my secretaries would be engaged in little else in the course of the day, and I would have no time for constructive work, but since I feel that you are men of genuine goodwill and your criticisms are sincerely set forth, I would like to answer your statement in what I hope will be patient and reasonable terms.

I think I should give the reason for my
being in Birmingham, since you have
been influenced by the argument of
"outsiders coming in." I have the honor
of serving as president of the Southern
Christian Leadership Conference,
an organization operating in every
Southern state, with headquarters
in Atlanta, Georgia. We have some
eighty-five affiliate organizations
all across the South—one being the
Alabama Christian Movement for
Human Rights. Whenever necessary
and possible we share staff, educational

and financial resources with our affiliates. Several months ago our local affiliate here in Birmingham invited us to be on call to engage in a nonviolent direct action program if such were deemed necessary. We readily consented, and when the hour came we lived up to our promises. So I am here, along with several members of my staff, because we were invited here. I am here because I have basic organizational ties here.

Beyond this, I am in Birmingham because injustice is here. Just as the eighth-century prophets left their little villages and carried their "thus saith the Lord" far beyond the boundaries of their hometowns, and just as the Apostle Paul left his little village of Tarsus and carried the Gospel of Jesus Christ to practically every hamlet and city of the Graeco-Roman world, I too am compelled to carry the gospel of freedom beyond my particular hometown. Like Paul, I must constantly respond to the Macedonian call for aid.

Moreover, I am cognizant of the interrelatedness of all communities and states. I cannot sit idly by in Atlanta and not be concerned about what happens in Birmingham. Injustice anywhere is a threat to justice everywhere. We are caught in an inescapable network of mutuality, tied in a single garment of destiny. Whatever affects one directly affects all indirectly. Never again can we afford to live with the narrow, provincial "outside agitator" idea. Anyone who lives inside the United States can never be considered an outsider anywhere in this country.

You deplore the demonstrations that are presently taking place in Birmingham. But I am sorry that your statement did not express a similar concern for the conditions that brought the demonstrations into being. I am sure that each of you would want to go beyond the superficial social analyst who looks merely at effects and does not grapple with underlying causes. I would not hesitate to say that it is unfortunate that so-called demonstrations are taking place in Birmingham at this time, but I would say in even more emphatic terms that it is even more unfortunate that the white power structure of this city left the Negro community with no other alternative.

In any nonviolent campaign there are four basic steps: (1) Collection of the facts to determine whether injustices are alive. (2) Negotiation. (3) Self-purification and (4) Direct Action. We have gone through all of these steps in Birmingham. There can be no gainsaying of the fact that racial injustice engulfs this community. Birmingham is probably the most thoroughly segregated city in the United States. Its ugly record of police brutality is known in every section of this country. Its unjust treatment of Negroes in the courts is a notorious reality. There have been more unsolved bombings of Negro homes and churches in Birmingham than in any city in this nation. These are the hard, brutal, and unbelievable facts. On the basis of these conditions Negro leaders sought to negotiate with the city fathers. But the political leaders consistently refused to engage in good faith negotiation.

Then came the opportunity last September to talk with some of the leaders of the economic community. In these negotiating sessions certain promises were made by the merchants—such as the promise to remove the humiliating racial signs from the stores. On the basis of these promises Rev. Shuttlesworth and the leaders of the Alabama Christian Movement for Human Rights agreed to call a moratorium on any type of demonstration. As the weeks and months unfolded we realized we

were the victims of a broken promise.
The signs remained. Like so many
experiences of the past we were
confronted with blasted hopes, and the
dark shadow of a deep disappointment
settled upon us. So we had no
alternative except that of preparing
for direct action, whereby we would
present our very bodies as a means of
laying our case before the conscience of
the local and national community. We
were not unmindful of the difficulties
involved. So we decided to go through a
process of self-purification. We started

having workshops on nonviolence
and repeatedly asked ourselves the
questions, "Are you able to accept blows
without retaliating?" "Are you able to
endure the ordeals of jail?" We decided
to set our direct action program around
the Easter season, realizing that with
the exception of Christmas, this was the
largest shopping period of the year.
Knowing that a strong economic
withdrawal program would be the
by-product of direct action, we felt that
this was the best time to bring pressure
on the merchants for the needed

changes. Then it occurred to us that the March election was ahead, and so we speedily decided to postpone action until after election day. When we discovered that Mr. Connor was in the runoff, we decided again to postpone action so that the demonstrations could not be used to cloud the issues. At this time we agreed to begin our nonviolent witness the day after the runoff.

This reveals that we did not move irresponsibly into direct action. We too wanted to see Mr. Connor defeated; so we went through postponement after postponement to aid in this community need. After this we felt that direct action could be delayed no longer.

Creative Tension

You may well ask, "Why direct action? Why sit-ins, marches, etc.? Isn't negotiation a better path?" You are exactly right in your call for negotiation. Indeed, this is the purpose of direct action. Nonviolent direct action seeks to create such a crisis and establish such creative tension that a community that has constantly refused to negotiate is forced to confront the issue. It seeks to dramatize the issue so that it can no longer be ignored. I just referred to the creation of tension as a part of the work of the nonviolent resister. This may sound rather shocking. But I must confess that I am not afraid of the word "tension." I have earnestly worked and preached against violent tension, but there is a type of constructive nonviolent tension that is necessary for growth. Just as Socrates felt it was necessary to create a tension in the mind so that individuals could rise from the bondage of myths and half-truths to the unfettered realm of creative analysis and objective appraisal, we must see the need of having nonviolent gadflies to create the kind of tension in society that will help men to rise from the dark depths of prejudice and racism to the majestic heights of understanding and brotherhood. So the purpose of the direct action is to create a situation so crisis-packed that it will inevitably open the door to negotiation. We, therefore, concur with you in your call for negotiation. Too long has our beloved Southland been bogged down in the tragic attempt to live in monologue rather than dialogue.

One of the basic points in your statement is that our acts are untimely. Some have asked, "Why didn't you give the new administration time to act?" The only answer that I can give to this inquiry is that the new administration must be prodded about as much as the outgoing one before it acts. We will be sadly mistaken if we feel that the election of Mr. Boutwell will bring the millennium to Birmingham. While Mr. Boutwell is much more articulate and gentle than Mr. Connor, they are both segregationists, dedicated to the task of maintaining the status quo. The hope I see in Mr. Boutwell is that he will be reasonable enough to see the futility of massive resistance to desegregation. But he will not see this without pressure from the devotees of civil rights. My friends, I must say to you that we have not made a single gain in civil rights without determined legal and nonviolent pressure. History is the long and tragic story of the fact that privileged groups seldom give up their privileges voluntarily. Individuals

may see the moral light and voluntarily
give up their unjust posture, but as
Reinhold Niebuhr has reminded
us, groups are more immoral than
individuals.

We know through painful experience that freedom is never voluntarily given by the oppressor; it must be demanded by the oppressed. Frankly, I have never yet engaged in a direct action movement that was "well-timed" according to the timetable of those who have not suffered unduly from the disease of segregation. For years now I have heard the word "Wait!" It rings in the ear of every Negro with a piercing familiarity. This "wait" has almost always meant "never." It has been a tranquilizing thalidomide, relieving the emotional stress for a moment, only to give birth to an ill-formed infant of frustration. We must come to see with the distinguished jurist of yesterday that "justice too long delayed is justice denied." We have waited for more than three hundred and forty years for our constitutional and God-given rights. The nations of Asia and Africa are moving with jetlike speed toward the goal of political independence, and we still creep at horse-and-buggy pace toward the gaining of a cup of coffee at a lunch counter. I guess it is easy for those who have never felt the stinging darts of segregation to say, "Wait." But when you have seen vicious mobs lynch your mothers and fathers at will and drown your sisters and brothers at whim; when you have seen hate-filled policemen curse, kick, brutalize, and even kill your Black brothers and sisters with impunity; when you see the vast majority of your twenty million Negro brothers smothering in an airtight cage of poverty in the midst of an affluent society; when you suddenly find your tongue twisted and your speech stammering as you seek to explain to your six-year-old daughter why she can't go to the public amusement park that has just been advertised on television, and see tears welling up in her little eyes when she is told that Funtown is closed to colored children, and see the depressing clouds of inferiority begin to form in her little mental sky, and see her begin to distort her little personality by unconsciously developing a bitterness toward white people; when you have to concoct an answer for a five-year-old son asking in agonizing pathos: "Daddy, why do white people treat colored people so mean?";

when you take a cross-country drive and find it necessary to sleep night after night in the uncomfortable corners of your automobile because no motel will accept you; when you are humiliated day in and day out by nagging signs reading "white" and "colored"; when your first name becomes "nigger" and your middle name becomes "boy" (however old you are) and your last name becomes "John," and when your wife and mother are never given the respected title "Mrs."; when you are harried by day and haunted at night by the fact that you are a Negro, living constantly at tiptoe stance,

never quite knowing what to expect

next, and plagued with inner fears

and outer resentments; when you are

forever fighting a degenerating sense of

"nobodiness"; then you will understand

why we find it difficult to wait. There

comes a time when the cup of endurance

runs over, and men are no longer willing

to be plunged into an abyss of injustice

where they experience the blackness

of corroding despair. I hope, sirs, you

can understand our legitimate and

unavoidable impatience.

Breaking the Law

You express a great deal of anxiety
over our willingness to break laws.
This is certainly a legitimate concern.
Since we so diligently urge people to
obey the Supreme Court's decision
of 1954 outlawing segregation in the
public schools, it is rather strange and
paradoxical to find us consciously
breaking laws. One may well ask, "How
can you advocate breaking some laws
and obeying others?" The answer is
found in the fact that there are two

types of laws: there are <u>just</u> and there are <u>unjust</u> laws. I would agree with St. Augustine that "an unjust law is no law at all."

Now what is the difference between the two? How does one determine when a law is just or unjust? A just law is a man-made code that squares with the moral law or the law of God. An unjust law is a code that is out of harmony with the moral law. To put it in the terms of St. Thomas Aquinas, an unjust law is a human law that is not rooted in eternal and natural law. Any law that uplifts human personality is just. Any law that degrades human personality is unjust. All segregation statutes are unjust because segregation distorts the soul and damages the personality. It gives the segregator a false sense of superiority, and the segregated a false sense of inferiority. To use the words of Martin Buber, the great Jewish philosopher, segregation substitutes an "I-it" relationship for the "I-thou" relationship, and ends up relegating persons to the status of things. So segregation is not only politically, economically, and sociologically unsound but it is morally wrong and sinful. Paul Tillich has said that sin is separation. Isn't segregation an existential expression of man's tragic separation, an expression of his awful estrangement, his terrible sinfulness? So I can urge men to disobey segregation ordinances because they are morally wrong.

Let us turn to a more concrete example of just and unjust laws. An unjust law is a code that a majority inflicts on a minority that is not binding on itself. This is difference made legal. On the other hand a just law is a code that a majority compels a minority to follow that it is willing to follow itself. This is sameness made legal.

Let me give another explanation. An unjust law is a code inflicted upon a minority which that minority had no part in enacting or creating because they did not have the unhampered right to vote. Who can say that the legislature of Alabama which set up the segregation laws was democratically elected? Throughout the state of Alabama all types of conniving methods are used to prevent Negroes from becoming registered voters, and there are some counties without a single Negro registered to vote despite the fact that the Negro constitutes a majority of the population. Can any law set up in such a state be considered democratically structured?

These are just a few examples of unjust and just laws. There are some instances when a law is just on its face and unjust in its application. For instance, I was arrested Friday on a charge of parading without a permit. Now there is nothing wrong with an ordinance which requires a permit for a parade, but when the ordinance is used to preserve segregation and to deny citizens the First Amendment privilege of peaceful assembly and peaceful protest, then it becomes unjust.

I hope you can see the distinction I am trying to point out. In no sense do I advocate evading or defying the law as the rabid segregationist would do. This would lead to anarchy. One who breaks an unjust law must do it <u>openly</u>, <u>lovingly</u> (not hatefully as the white mothers did in New Orleans when they were seen on television screaming, "nigger, nigger, nigger"), and with a willingness to accept the penalty. I submit that an individual who breaks a law that conscience tells him is unjust, and willingly accepts the penalty by staying in jail to arouse the conscience of the community over its injustice, is in reality expressing the very highest respect for law.

Of course, there is nothing new about this kind of civil disobedience. It was seen sublimely in the refusal of Shadrach, Meshach, and Abednego to obey the laws of Nebuchadnezzar because a higher moral law was involved. It was practiced superbly by the early Christians who were willing to face hungry lions and the excruciating pain of chopping blocks before submitting to certain unjust laws of the Roman empire. To a degree academic freedom is a reality today because Socrates practiced civil disobedience.

The White Moderate

We can never forget that everything
Hitler did in Germany was "legal,"
and everything the Hungarian
freedom fighters did in Hungary was
"illegal." It was "illegal" to aid and
comfort a Jew in Hitler's Germany.
But I am sure that if I had lived in
Germany during that time I would
have aided and comforted my Jewish
brothers even though it was illegal.
If I lived in a Communist country
today where certain principles dear

to the Christian faith are suppressed,
I believe I would openly advocate
disobeying these anti-religious laws.

I must make two honest confessions to you, my Christian and Jewish brothers. First, I must confess that over the last few years I have been gravely disappointed with the white moderate. I have almost reached the regrettable conclusion that the Negro's great stumbling block in the stride toward freedom is not the White Citizen's Councilor or the Ku Klux Klanner, but the white moderate who is more devoted to "order" than to justice; who prefers a negative peace, which is the absence of tension, to a positive peace, which is the presence of justice;

who constantly says, "I agree with you in the goal you seek, but I can't agree with your methods of direct action"; who paternalistically feels that he can set the timetable for another man's freedom; who lives by the myth of time; and who constantly advises the Negro to wait until a "more convenient season." Shallow understanding from people of goodwill is more frustrating than absolute misunderstanding from people of ill will. Lukewarm acceptance is much more bewildering than outright rejection.

I had hoped that the white moderate would understand that law and order exist for the purpose of establishing justice, and that when they fail to do this they become dangerously structured dams that block the flow of social progress. I had hoped that the white moderate would understand that the present tension in the South is merely a necessary phase of the transition from an obnoxious negative peace, where the Negro passively accepted his unjust plight, to a substance-filled positive peace, where all men will respect the dignity and worth of human personality. Actually, we who engage in nonviolent direct action are not the creators of tension. We merely bring to the surface the hidden tension that is already alive. We bring it out in the open, where it can be seen and dealt with. Like a boil that can never be cured as long as it is covered up but must be opened with all its pus-flowing ugliness to the natural medicines of air and light, injustice must likewise be exposed, with all of the tension its exposing creates, to the light of human conscience and the air of national opinion before it can be cured.

In your statement you asserted that our actions, even though peaceful, must be condemned because they precipitate violence. But can this assertion be logically made? Isn't this like condemning the robbed man because his possession of money precipitated the evil act of robbery? Isn't this like condemning Socrates because his unswerving commitment to truth and his philosophical delvings precipitated the misguided popular mind to make him drink the hemlock? Isn't this like condemning Jesus because His unique

God-consciousness and never-ceasing devotion to His will precipitated the evil act of crucifixion? We must come to see, as federal courts have consistently affirmed, that it is immoral to urge an individual to withdraw his efforts to gain his basic constitutional rights because the quest precipitates violence. Society must protect the robbed and punish the robber.

I had also hoped that the white moderate would reject the myth of time. I received a letter this morning from a white brother in Texas which said: "All Christians know that the colored people will receive equal rights eventually, but it is possible that you are in too great of a religious hurry. It has taken Christianity almost 2000 years to accomplish what it has. The teachings of Christ take time to come to earth." All that is said here grows out of a tragic misconception of time. It is the strangely irrational notion that there is something in the very flow of time that will inevitably cure all ills. Actually time is neutral. It can be used either destructively or constructively. I am coming to feel that the people of ill will have used time much more effectively than the people of goodwill. We will have to repent in this generation not merely for the vitriolic words and actions of the bad people but for the appalling silence of the good people. We must come to see that human progress never rolls in on wheels of inevitability. It comes through the tireless efforts and persistent work of men willing to be co-workers with God, and without this hard work time itself becomes an ally of the forces of social stagnation. We must use time creatively, and forever realize that the time is always ripe to do right. Now is the time to make real the promise of democracy, and transform our pending national elegy into a creative psalm of brotherhood. Now is the time to lift our national policy from the quicksand of racial injustice to the solid rock of human dignity.

You spoke of our activity in Birmingham as extreme. At first I was rather disappointed that fellow clergymen would see my nonviolent efforts as those of the extremist. I started thinking about the fact that I stand in the middle of two opposing forces in the Negro community. One is a force of complacency, made up of Negroes who, as a result of long years of oppression, have been so completely drained of self-respect and a sense of "somebodiness" that they have adjusted to segregation, and of a few Negroes in the middle class who, because of a degree of academic and economic security, and because at points they profit by segregation, have unconsciously become insensitive to the problems of the masses. The other force is one of bitterness and hatred and comes perilously close to advocating violence. It is expressed in the various Black Nationalist groups that are springing up over the nation, the largest and best known being Elijah Muhammad's Muslim movement. This movement is nourished by the contemporary frustration over the continued existence of racial discrimination. It is made up of people who have lost faith in America, who have absolutely repudiated Christianity, and who have concluded that the white man is an incurable "devil." I have tried to stand between these two forces, saying that we need not follow the "do-nothingism" of the complacent or the hatred and despair of the Black Nationalist. There is the more excellent way of love and nonviolent protest. I'm grateful to God that, through the Negro church, the dimension of nonviolence entered our struggle. If this philosophy had not emerged, I am convinced that by now many streets of the South would be flowing with floods of blood. And I am further convinced that if our white brothers dismiss as "rabble-rousers" and "outside agitators" those of us who are working through the channels of nonviolent direct action and refuse to support our nonviolent efforts, millions of Negroes, out of frustration and despair, will seek solace and security in Black Nationalist ideologies, a development that will lead inevitably to a frightening racial nightmare.

Oppressed people cannot remain oppressed forever. The urge for freedom will eventually come. This is what has happened to the American Negro. Something within has reminded him of his birthright of freedom; something without has reminded him that he can gain it. Consciously and unconsciously, he has been swept in by what the Germans call the "Zeitgeist," and with his Black brothers of Africa, and his brown and yellow brothers of Asia, South America, and the Caribbean, he is moving with a sense of cosmic urgency toward the promised land of racial justice. Recognizing this vital urge that has engulfed the Negro community, one should readily understand public demonstrations. The Negro has many pent-up resentments and latent frustrations. He has to get them out. So let him march sometime; let him have his prayer pilgrimages to the city hall; understand why he must have sit-ins and freedom rides. If his repressed emotions do not come out in these nonviolent ways, they will come out in ominous expressions of violence.

This is not a threat; it is a fact of history. So I have not said to my people, "Get rid of your discontent." But I have tried to say that this normal and healthy discontent can be channelized through the creative outlet of nonviolent direct action. Now this approach is being dismissed as extremist. I must admit that I was initially disappointed in being so categorized.

Extremists for Love

But as I continued to think about the matter I gradually gained a bit of satisfaction from being considered an extremist. Was not Jesus an extremist in love—"Love your enemies, bless them that curse you, pray for them that despitefully use you." Was not Amos an extremist for justice—"Let justice roll down like waters and righteousness like a mighty stream." Was not Paul an extremist for the Gospel of Jesus Christ—"I bear in my body the marks of the Lord Jesus." Was not Martin

Luther an extremist—"Here I stand; I can do none other so help me God." Was not John Bunyan an extremist—"I will stay in jail to the end of my days before I make a butchery of my conscience." Was not Abraham Lincoln an extremist—"This nation cannot survive half slave and half free." Was not Thomas Jefferson an extremist—"We hold these truths to be self-evident, that all men are created equal." So the question is not whether we will be extremists, but what kind of extremists will we be. Will we be extremists for hate, or will we be extremists for love? Will we be extremists for the preservation of injustice—or will we be extremists for the cause of justice? In that dramatic scene on Calvary's hill, three men were crucified. We must not forget that all three men were crucified for the same crime—the crime of extremism. Two were extremists for immorality, and thusly fell below their environment. The other, Jesus Christ, was an extremist for love, truth, and goodness, and thereby rose above his environment. So, after all, maybe the South, the nation, and the world are in dire need of creative extremists.

I had hoped that the white moderate would see this. Maybe I was too optimistic. Maybe I expected too much. I guess I should have realized that few members of a race that has oppressed another race can understand or appreciate the deep groans and passionate yearnings of those that have been oppressed, and still fewer have the vision to see that injustice must be rooted out by strong, persistent, and determined action. I am thankful, however, that some of our white brothers have grasped the meaning of this social revolution and committed themselves to it. They are still too small in quantity, but they are big in quality. Some like Ralph McGill, Lillian Smith, Harry Golden, and James Dabbs have written about our struggle in eloquent, prophetic, and understanding terms. Others have marched with us down nameless streets of the South. They have languished in filthy roach-infested jails, suffering the abuse and brutality of angry policemen who see them as "dirty nigger lovers." They, unlike so many of their moderate brothers and sisters, have recognized the urgency of the moment and sensed the need for powerful "action" antidotes to combat the disease of segregation.

The White Church

Let me rush on to mention my
other disappointment. I have been
so greatly disappointed with the
white church and its leadership.
Of course, there are some notable
exceptions. I am not unmindful of
the fact that each of you has taken
some significant stands on this issue.
I commend you, Rev. Stallings, for
your Christian stand on this past
Sunday, in welcoming Negroes

to your worship service on a
nonsegregated basis. I commend
the Catholic leaders of this state for
integrating Springhill College several
years ago.

But despite these notable exceptions I must honestly reiterate that I have been disappointed with the church. I do not say that as one of those negative critics who can always find something wrong with the church. I say it as a minister of the gospel, who loves the church; who was nurtured in its bosom; who has been sustained by its spiritual blessings; and who will remain true to it as long as the cord of life shall lengthen.

I had the strange feeling when I was suddenly catapulted into the leadership of the bus protest in Montgomery several years ago that we would have the support of the white church. I felt that the white ministers, priests, and rabbis of the South would be some of our strongest allies. Instead, some have been outright opponents, refusing to understand the freedom movement and misrepresenting its leaders; all too many others have been more cautious than courageous and have remained silent behind the anesthetizing security of the stained-glass windows.

In spite of my shattered dreams of the past, I came to Birmingham with the hope that the white religious leadership of this community would see the justice of our cause, and with deep moral concern, serve as the channel through which our just grievances would get to the power structure. I had hoped that each of you would understand. But again I have been disappointed.

I have heard numerous religious leaders of the South call upon their worshippers to comply with a desegregation decision because it is the <u>law</u>, but I have longed to hear white ministers say, "Follow this decree because integration is morally <u>right</u> and the Negro is your brother." In the midst of blatant injustices inflicted upon the Negro, I have watched white churches stand on the sideline and merely mouth pious irrelevancies and sanctimonious trivialities. In the midst of a mighty struggle to rid our nation of racial and economic injustice, I have heard so many ministers say, "Those are social issues with which the Gospel has no real concern," and I have watched so many churches commit themselves to a completely otherworldly religion which made a strange distinction between body and soul, the sacred and the secular.

So here we are moving toward the exit
of the twentieth century with a religious
community largely adjusted to the
status quo, standing as a taillight behind
other community agencies rather than
a headlight leading men to higher levels
of justice.

I have travelled the length and breadth of Alabama, Mississippi, and all the other Southern states. On sweltering summer days and crisp autumn mornings I have looked at her beautiful churches with their lofty spires pointing heavenward. I have beheld the impressive outlay of her massive religious education buildings. Over and over again I have found myself asking: "What kind of people worship here? Who is their God? Where were their voices when the lips of Governor Barnett dripped with words of interposition and nullification? Where were they when Governor Wallace gave the clarion call for defiance and hatred? Where were their voices of support when tired, bruised, and weary Negro men and women decided to rise from the dark dungeons of complacency to the bright hills of creative protest?"

Yes, these questions are still in my mind. In deep disappointment, I have wept over the laxity of the church. But be assured that my tears have been tears of love. There can be no deep disappointment where there is not deep love. Yes, I love the church; I love her sacred walls. How could I do otherwise? I am in the rather unique position of being the son, the grandson, and the great-grandson of preachers. Yes, I see the church as the body of Christ. But, oh! How we have blemished and scarred that body through social neglect and fear of being nonconformists.

Disturbers of the Peace

There was a time when the church was very powerful. It was during that period when the early Christians rejoiced when they were deemed worthy to suffer for what they believed. In those days the church was not merely a thermometer that recorded the ideas and principles of popular opinion; it was a thermostat that transformed the mores of society. Whenever the early Christians entered a town the power structure got disturbed and immediately sought to convict them for being "disturbers of the peace" and "outside agitators." But they went on with the conviction that they were "a colony of heaven," and had to obey God rather than man. They were small in number but big in commitment. They were too God-intoxicated to be "astronomically intimidated." They brought an end to such ancient evils as infanticide and gladiatorial contests.

Things are different now. The contemporary church is often a weak, ineffectual voice with an uncertain sound. It is so often the arch supporter of the status quo. Far from being disturbed by the presence of the church, the power structure of the average community is consoled by the church's silent and often vocal sanction of things as they are.

But the judgment of God is upon
the church as never before. If the
church of today does not recapture the
sacrificial spirit of the early church, it
will lose its authentic ring, forfeit the
loyalty of millions, and be dismissed
as an irrelevant social club with no
meaning for the twentieth century. I am
meeting young people every day whose
disappointment with the church has
risen to outright disgust.

Maybe again I have been too optimistic. Is organized religion too inextricably bound to the status quo to save our nation and the world? Maybe I must turn my faith to the inner spiritual church, the church within the church, as the true <u>ecclesia</u> and the hope of the world. But again I am thankful to God that some noble souls from the ranks of organized religion have broken loose from the paralyzing chains of conformity and joined us as active partners in the struggle for freedom. They have left their secure congregations and walked the streets of Albany, Georgia, with us. They have gone through the highways of the South on tortuous rides for freedom. Yes, they have gone to jail with us. Some have been kicked out of their churches, and lost support of their bishops and fellow ministers. But they have gone with the faith that right defeated is stronger than evil triumphant. These men have been the leaven in the lump of the race. Their witness has been the spiritual salt that has preserved the true meaning of the Gospel in these troubled times. They have carved a tunnel of hope through the dark mountain of disappointment.

I hope the church as a whole will meet the challenge of this decisive hour. But even if the church does not come to the aid of justice, I have no despair about the future. I have no fear about the outcome of our struggle in Birmingham, even if our motives are presently misunderstood. We will reach the goal of freedom in Birmingham and all over the nation, because the goal of America is freedom. Abused and scorned though we may be, our destiny is tied up with the destiny of America. Before the pilgrims landed

at Plymouth we were here. Before
the pen of Jefferson etched across the
pages of history the majestic words of
the Declaration of Independence, we
were here. For more than two centuries
our fore-parents labored here without
wages; they made cotton king; and
they built the homes of their masters
in the midst of brutal injustice and
shameful humiliation—and yet out of
a bottomless vitality they continued to
thrive and develop. If the inexpressible
cruelties of slavery could not stop us, the
opposition we now face will surely fail.

We will win our freedom because the sacred heritage of our nation and the eternal will of God are embodied in our echoing demands.

Bull Connor's Police

I must close now. But before closing I am impelled to mention one other point in your statement that troubled me profoundly. You warmly commended the Birmingham police force for keeping "order" and "preventing violence." I don't believe you would have so warmly commended the police force if you had seen its angry, violent dogs literally biting six unarmed, nonviolent Negroes. I don't believe you would so quickly commend the policemen if you would observe their ugly and inhuman treatment of Negroes here in the city jail; if you would watch them push and curse old Negro women and young Negro girls; if you would see them slap and kick old Negro men and young boys; if you will observe them, as they did on two occasions, refuse to give us food because we wanted to sing our grace together. I'm sorry that I can't join you in your praise for the police department.

It is true that they have been rather disciplined in their public handling of the demonstrators. In this sense they have been rather publicly "nonviolent." But for what purpose? To preserve the evil system of segregation. Over the last few years I have consistently preached that nonviolence demands that the means we use must be as pure as the ends we seek. So I have tried to make it clear that it is wrong to use immoral means to attain moral ends. But now I must affirm that it is just as wrong, or even more so, to use moral

means to preserve immoral ends.
Maybe Mr. Connor and his policemen
have been rather publicly nonviolent,
as Chief Pritchett was in Albany,
Georgia, but they have used the moral
means of nonviolence to maintain the
immoral end of flagrant racial injustice.
T. S. Eliot has said that there is no
greater treason than to do the right
deed for the wrong reason.

I wish to commend the Negro sit-inners
and demonstrators of Birmingham for
their sublime courage, their willingness
to suffer, and their amazing discipline
in the midst of the most inhuman
provocation. One day the South will
recognize its real heroes. They will
be the James Merediths, courageously
and with a majestic sense of purpose
facing jeering and hostile mobs and the
agonizing loneliness that characterizes
the life of the pioneer. They will be
old, oppressed, battered Negro women,
symbolized in a seventy-two-year-old

woman of Montgomery, Alabama, who rose up with a sense of dignity and with her people decided not to ride the segregated buses, and responded to one who inquired about her tiredness with ungrammatical profundity: "My feet is tired, but my soul is rested." They will be the young high school and college students, young ministers of the Gospel, and a host of their elders courageously and nonviolently sitting in at lunch counters and willingly going to jail for conscience's sake. One day the South will know that when these disinherited children of God sat down at lunch counters they were in reality standing up for the best in the American dream and the most sacred values in our Judeo-Christian heritage and, thusly, carrying our whole nation back to those great wells of democracy which were dug deep by the founding fathers in the formulation of the Constitution and the Declaration of Independence.

Never before have I written a letter this long (or should I say a book?). I'm afraid that it is much too long to take your precious time. I can assure you that it would have been much shorter if I had been writing from a comfortable desk, but what else is there to do when you are alone for days in the dull monotony of a narrow jail cell other than write long letters, think strange thoughts, and pray long prayers?

If I have said anything in this letter that is an overstatement of the truth and is indicative of an unreasonable impatience, I beg you to forgive me. If I have said anything in this letter that is an understatement of the truth and is indicative of my having a patience that makes me patient with anything less than brotherhood, I beg God to forgive me.

I hope this letter finds you strong in the faith. I also hope that circumstances will soon make it possible for me to meet each of you, not as an integrationist or a civil rights leader but as a fellow clergyman and a Christian brother. Let us all hope that the dark clouds of racial prejudice will soon pass away, and the deep fog of misunderstanding will be lifted from our fear-drenched communities, and in some not too distant tomorrow the radiant stars of love and brotherhood will shine

over our great nation with all their
scintillating beauty.

Yours for the cause of Peace
and Brotherhood
Martin Luther King Jr.

About the Author

Dr. Martin Luther King Jr. (1929–1968), civil rights leader and recipient of the Nobel Prize for Peace, inspired and sustained the struggle for freedom, nonviolence, interracial brotherhood, and social justice.

Afterword

I first read "Letter from Birmingham Jail" in solitary confinement. The first phrase of Dr. Martin Luther King Jr.'s letter unsettled me: "While confined here in the Birmingham City Jail."

I was halfway through a prison sentence that seemed bent on driving me insane. The two fights I'd lost without throwing a good punch suggested that I was nonviolent. But my nonviolence had always been borne out of fear. I still barely weighed 120 pounds. And I feared discovering the other side of letting go of the rage swelling inside me. Every day I was inside, I was afraid of something new. I knew prison was the place of the disposed and the unworthy.

As difficult as prison was, I cried only twice. The first, on December 9, 1996, a month after my sixteenth birthday, after I had just confessed to carjacking a man asleep in his car and attempting to carjack two women. My lawyer had explained to me that I might get life in prison. I leaned my 125 pounds against the cold bars of a cell in a Virginia jail and could not stop crying for all that I imagined I was losing.

I cried because a judge had remanded me into the custody of the state, which meant that my regular nightly routine of going to get my mother a glass of water before she slept would not be done again for a period of time I was not brave enough to contemplate.

The second time, a year later, I was on the top bunk, and under me was a Puerto Rican kid whose name I no longer remember but whose state number I do: 251532. My state number was 251534, and his was a pace before mine, an accident of order more than anything else, but one that meant he entered the cell moments before me and claimed the bottom bunk, a gift I'd later realize as I listened to a run of public radio shows about the Civil Rights Movement that day.

Though I'd grown up on a steady diet of *Eyes on the Prize*, the Civil Rights Movement was more historical artifact than living history. What I learned about the past stayed locked in answers on quizzes, essays, or the word searches that were the staples of MLK Day and Black History Month. Yet while listening to those radio shows recount the story of Dr. Martin Luther King Jr., I could not stop myself from weeping.

This is what I thought while listening to the stories of the Edmund Pettus Bridge and the Montgomery bus boycott and every way that the threat of incarceration had been used to try to quell their fight for justice: I'd ruined my life over a willingness to hurt somebody over a want to own what did not belong to me. Over trinkets. Over nothing.

Feeling like you've ruined your life is not the powerful motivator it might seem in retrospect. Mostly, I just felt afraid and unworthy of the so many freedoms I'd callously abandoned. There are no ways to open a prison cell from the inside. And once inside, it is impossible to answer your mother's call, whether she wants you to get her a glass of water or just wants to know that you are safe.

———

Most of us who have found ourselves in prisons in this country have not been the victims of a broken promise. Dr. Martin Luther King Jr. spent eight days in the Birmingham jail for "parading without a permit," for daring to say, as he did in the letter, that those who questioned him would understand why it was easy for him to advocate breaking unjust laws. While in a prison cell, he wrote, riffing on St. Thomas Aquinas, "A just law is a man-made code that squares with the moral law or the law of God."

Dr. King's letter, though directly a message to white moderates, became the message that I needed to hear, nearly fifty years later. The degrading sense of "nobodiness" that I was fighting had very little to do with the white infrastructure around me. If there were an abyss of despair that threatened to consume me, that abyss was filled with the threats that I'd made to boys and men whose skin was as brown as mine, to the threats that I heard those same men around me launch into the air.

Time is a funny thing. In my mind, the space

between King's "Letter from Birmingham Jail" and Bloody Sunday is a matter of moments, and not two years. I learned Dr. Martin Luther King Jr. wasn't on the bridge during Bloody Sunday, but two days later he crossed the bridge with hundreds of civil rights workers to say that we are not afraid—of the batons, the dogs, the rage, or even the deep fall into the awaiting water. On the 111th anniversary of the birthday of Rosa Parks, I walked in a downpour across the Edmund Pettus Bridge.

I'd spent forty minutes in a car with a white woman, driving to the bridge from Montgomery, Alabama, where, with my team from Freedom Reads,* I'd just

---

* Freedom Reads is the organization I created in 2020 to confront what prison does to the spirit. We open beautiful, handcrafted Freedom Libraries, which contain Dr. Martin Luther King Jr.'s "Letter from Birmingham Jail," in cellblocks in prisons all over the country.

visited the National Memorial for Peace and Justice. Conceptualized and created by Bryan Stevenson, the memorial is an almost countless number of COR-TEN steel pillars, each with the names and the dates of the people who had been lynched (if available) and the counties in the United State where the lynchings had been perpetrated. The pillars are overwhelming, and without intending to, I began to search for my name. The steel pillars seemed to fall from the sky. I nearly fell to my knees when I found my father's surname, Betts, on two Mississippi pillars. My father, whose name I share, has never told me where our people are from, and in a second, the history of the Great Migration became, for me, also a story of the Betts men who did not make it.

King confessed at the start of his letter that he would accomplish little if he sought to answer all the criticisms that crossed his desk. I must admit that the only criticism I've struggled in this life to answer comes far more from me than the world. Men I love have killed on purpose and by accident, have pulled pistols on lovers and enemies, and have sliced open the faces of peers for everything and for nothing. King answered these white clergymen because he believed them to be "men of genuine goodwill" with criticisms "sincerely set forth."

My friends and I, and many of the men and women I've encountered in prisons, understand ourselves to be the antithesis of Dr. Martin Luther King Jr. Our violence, intentional or not, reminds the world that we sought a perverse justice. And we carry hurt with us, wondering if we deserve something more than the ways we beat ourselves up.

I survived prison because I wanted, desperately, not to have to remember myself as a broken kid who ruined his life with a pistol. Survival forced me to see something that mattered in the men around me. They became my confidants, my friends. But surviving does not teach you that there is a place in the world for you. And maybe this is the point. King's "Letter from Birmingham Jail" is as thorough a disabusing of silence and sitting on the sidelines that a person might read. But it is also an admission that the project of this country has always been built on mercy. And maybe this is the point that I've been struggling for so many years to believe, the idea that I've struggled to hear. And so I return, again, to a sentence that captures a sentiment that runs through this letter, believing that, then and now, Birmingham is a metaphor for suffering everywhere, and also for the possibility of justice: "We will reach the goal of freedom in Birmingham and all over the nation, because the goal of America is freedom."

—Reginald Dwayne Betts

About Reginald Dwayne Betts

Reginald Dwayne Betts is a poet and lawyer. A 2021 MacArthur Fellow, he is the founder and CEO of Freedom Reads, an organization that makes beautifully handcrafted wooden bookcases and transforms them into libraries opened in prison cellblocks. The author of a memoir and four collections of poetry, he has transformed the American Book Award–winning *Felon* into a solo theater show that explores the post-incarceration experience and lingering consequences of a criminal record through poetry, stories, and engaging with the timeless and transcendental art of papermaking. Betts holds a JD from Yale Law School.